Because I AM Intelligent 365 Affirmations To Brighten Up Your Day

AMIRE BEN SALMI

aka

"Mr Because I Am Intelligent"

ISBN: 1912547023
ISBN-13: 978-1912547029

DEDICATION

I want to dedicate this book to
YOU
because
YOU are INTELLIGENT too.

To my mum and dad **Sabrina and Mohamed Ben Salmi** and to my brothers and sisters:
Lashai Ben Salmi (17yr old)
aka Lashai Ben Salmi My Journey,
Tray-Sean Ben Salmi (13yr old)
aka I'm That KID & 10 Seconds To Child Genius,
Yasmine Ben Salmi (10yr old**),**
aka LovePrenure,
Paolo Ben Salmi (8yr old)
aka Pint Size Adventurer.
Mary Paul my Nan Founder of Mary Paul's Creations.
Philip Chan aka 10 Seconds Maths Expert for believing in me and helping us to share our books with the world.

CONTENTS

FOREWORD

Because I AM Intelligent – 365 Affirmations To Brighten Up Your Day is an inspirational book of affirmations by my amazing 4 year old brother Amire.

Each time I observe my brother recite his 365 affirmations it warms my heart. I'm the eldest of five siblings and they never stop amazing me, especially Amire.

He's only 4, however he's extremely intelligent.

As an Andy Harrington ACE Mentor, a HSF-YLS (Harry Singha Foundation Young Leaders Summit) Lead Coach, author and public speaker I'm constantly surrounded by amazing individuals.

I truly believe that children have a lot to teach, if we are willing to listen. When my brother told me he was going to write this book I was beyond excited and told him that I'd love to write his book foreword.

Because I AM Intelligent – 365 Affirmations To Brighten Up Your Day is an inspirational book of affirmations, is truly an amazing read!

I honestly believe that Amire was the perfect person to write this book because of the fact that he has developed such an positive mind-set and attitude at such a young age and that is truly inspiring to kids of all ages.

I really believe that all kids should have a way of reminding themselves how powerful they are & that they also have the power to be, do and have whatever they desire, so long as the put their mind to! I would defiantly say that this book is very unique, in the fact that that kids will truly be able to relate to each and every affirmation.

Within this book you will find a range of fun, empowering & inspiring affirmations that will make sure that you feel empowered, inspired and filled with energy throughout the day

I truly believe that a positive and empowering mind-set can really make the biggest difference and if that can be seeded at a young age it will really allow a child to truly believe that the possibilities in life are limitless!

Like I mentioned earlier I really and truly believe that every child should have access to this book, for them to have a way of reminding themselves how amazing, powerful and unique they are.

I was felt really honored and delighted when Amire asked me to write his forward because I cannot put into words how important I believe it is that the future generations understand their power.

Lashai Ben Salmi

U.K 17 year old Youth Advocate, Winner of Regan Hillyer International Scholarship, Multi-award winning Author, Public Speaker, Andy Harrington ACE Coach, PRECIOUS Award, BYA Award, Harry Singha Foundation Lead Coach, Photographer, Videographer, Business/Personal Development Consultant and YouTuber 12K plus subscribers

ACKNOWLEDGMENTS

Thank you so much to everyone who has helped me and my family.

Thank you to our family's publisher
Mayooran Senthimani,

Published by

DVG STAR Publishing

Our family's graphic designer
PRASANTHIKA MIHIRANI.

You can find her on Facebook as

Swiss Graphics

365 Affirmations - To Brighten Up Your Day

I AM INTELLIGENT

I AM TALENTED

I AM LOVED

I AM GIFTED

I AM SPECIAL

I AM HAPPY

I AM A BOOK WORM

I AM LIVING THE DREAM NOW

I AM AN INVESTOR

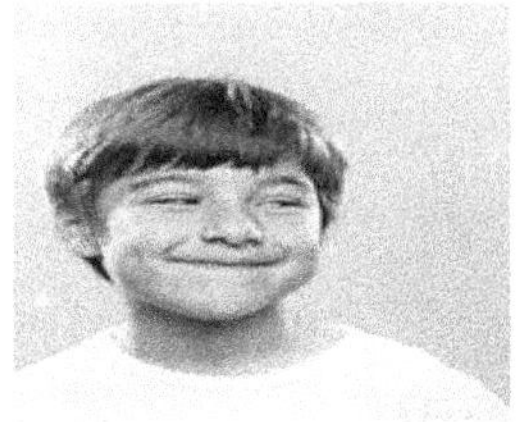

I AM LOVELY

I LOVE USING MY IMAGINATION TO DREAM BIG

I AM A CHILD GENIUS

I AM PEACE

I AM HOPE

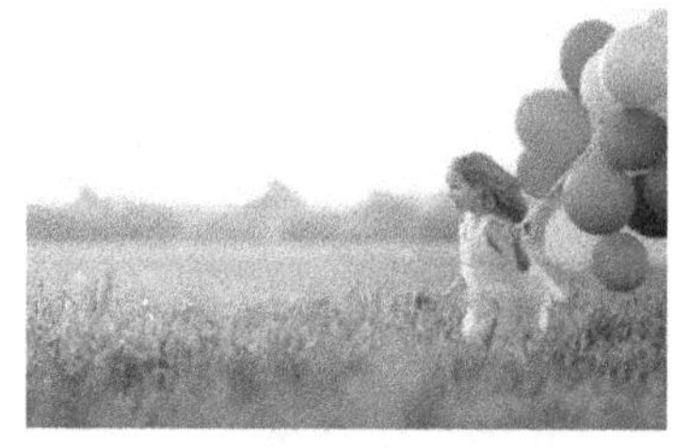

I AM ME

I LOVE MY LIFE

I LOVE MYSELF

I AM GOOD AT SAVING

I AM FREE

I AM PLAYFUL

I AM KIND

I AM LOVABLE

I AM CHOOSING TO BE PRESENT

I AM CHOOSING TO BE IN THE CHOICE

I AM CREATIVE

I AM COOL

I AM ALL KINDS OF AWESOME

I AM GRATEFUL FOR MY HEALTH

I AM LEARNING

I AM A STAR

I AM GROWING

I AM A CREATOR

I AM HELPFUL

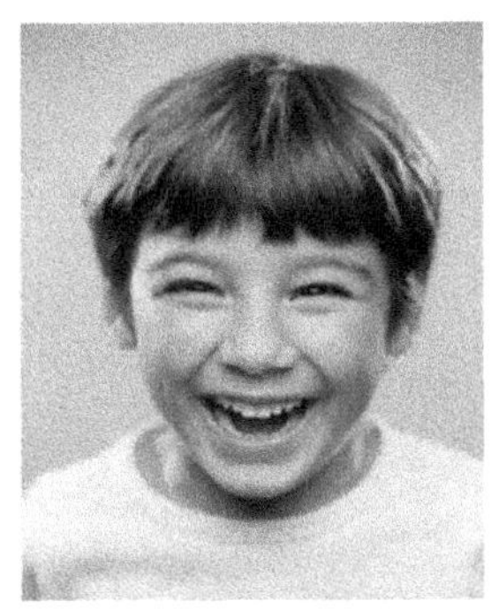

I AM FUNNY

I AM CLEVER

I AM PRESENT

I AM BRAVE

I ENJOY EXPLORING

I AM EXCITED

I AM ADVENTUROUS

I AM DOING MY BEST AND THAT IS GOOD ENOUGH

I AM TAKING ONE STEP AT A TIME

I AM A MASTERPIECE

I AM PLANTING A SEED FOR MY FUTURE

I AM LOVED AND APPRECIATED

I AM GRATEFUL

I LOVE MY FAMILY

I LOVE MY FRIENDS

I AM A WONDERFUL MASTERPIECE

I LOVE ANIMALS

I LOVE NATURE

I LOVE TO KEEP MY HOME TIDY WITH MY FAMILY

I AM THANKFUL

I AM ABUNDANT IN ALL AREAS OF MY LIFE

I AM ENJOYING MY DANCE WITH LIFE

I AM THE CAPTAIN OF MY SHIP

I AM CHOOSING POSITIVE ACTIONS AND WORDS

I AM IN ALIGNMENT

I AM CHOOSING TO BE HAPPY NOW

I AM GRATEFUL FOR MY FAMILY & FRIENDS

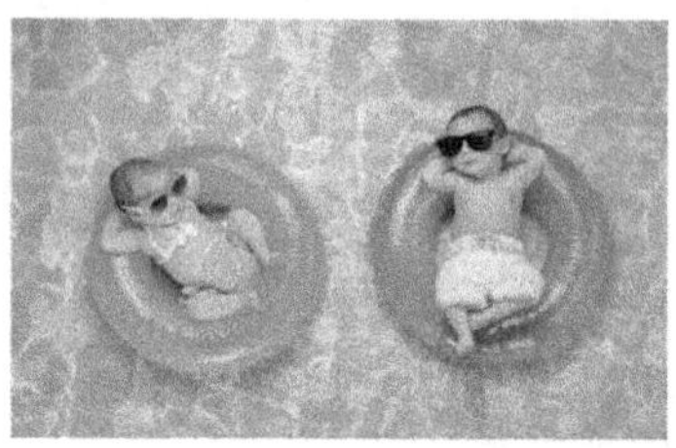

I AM RELAXED

I AM PEACEFUL

I AM A GOOD GIVER

I AM A GOOD RECEIVER

I AM A MONEY MAGNET

I AM CHOOSING TO EMBRACE LIFE

I AM SURROUNDED BY AMAZING MENTORS

I AM CURIOUS

I AM CAPABLE

I AM A GOOD LISTENER

I AM SURROUNDED BY LOVE

I AM DOING THE BEST I CAN

I AM A LEADER

I AM A CHAMPION

I AM LIVING THE DREAM

I AM ABLE

I AM THE INSPIRATION

I AM BEAUTIFUL

I AM AN OPPORTUNITY MAGNET

I AM STRONG

I AM HONEST

I AM TRUTHFUL

I AM MAGNIFICENT

I AM CHEERFUL

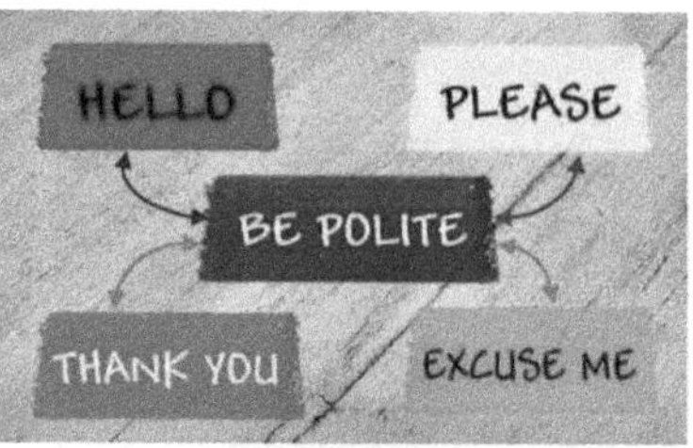

I AM RESPECTFUL

I AM A GOOD FRIEND

I APPRECIATE WHAT I HAVE

I AM PRECIOUS, AND SO ARE YOU

I AM THE KEY TO THE DOOR OF OPPORTUNITIES

I HAVE POSITIVE THOUGHTS

I HAVE THE POWER TO CHANGE THE WORLD WITH OTHERS

I CAN BE, DO & HAVE WHATEVER I DESIRE

EVERYDAY IS A NEW ADVENTURE

I LOVE SMILING

I LOVE CUDDLES

I AM FORGIVING

I AM WORTHY

I SHOW OTHERS THAT I CARE

I WORK SMART, NOT HARD

I AM ALWAYS OPEN TO LEARNING NEW THINGS

I AM GRATEFUL FOR WHAT I ACHIEVE IN MY LIFE

I LOVE LEARNING

I AM VALUED

I WAS BORN READY

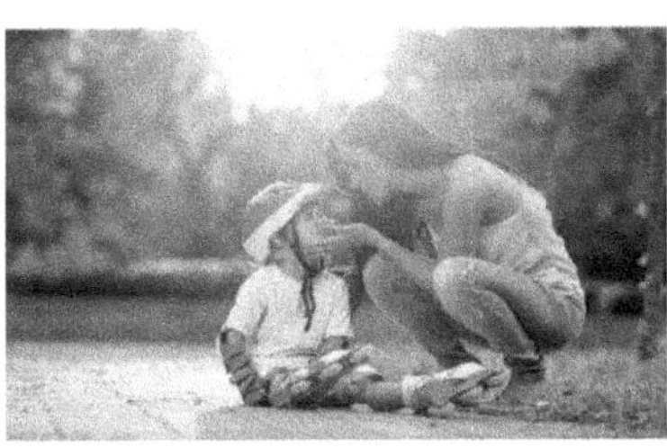

**WHEN I FALL,
I GET BACK UP**

I LEARN FROM MY MISTAKES

I AM CREATING MORE PROSPERITY

I AM CONFIDENT

I AM SURROUNDED BY PEOPLE THAT LOVE ME

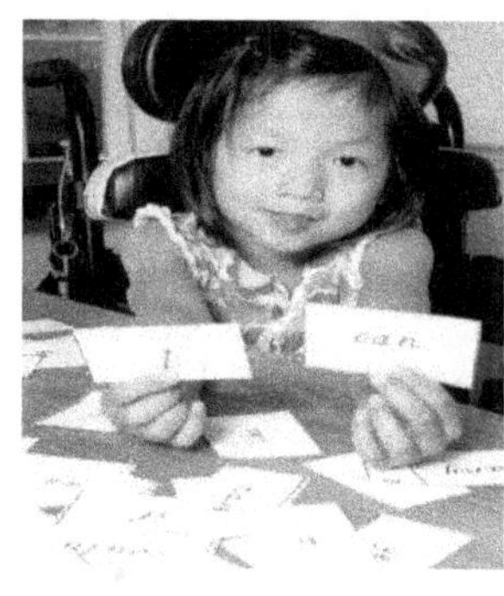

I CAN DO IT

I AM AMAZING JUST THE WAY I AM

I ALWAYS ASK QUESTIONS

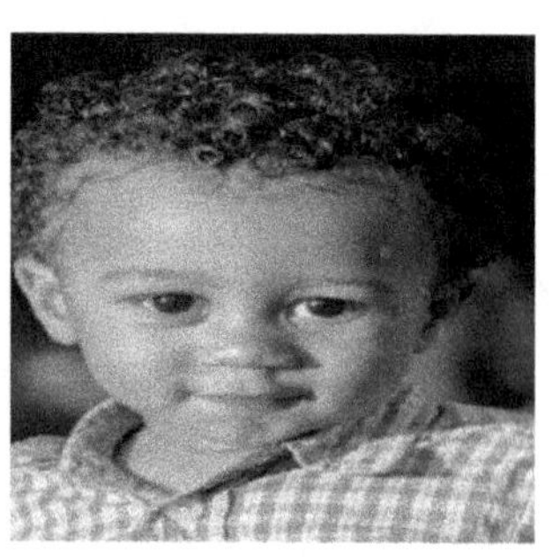

I WAS BORN AMAZING

I AM THE PERSON WHO CAN LIGHT UP YOUR DAY

I ENJOY HELPING OTHERS

I LOVE TO MAKE NEW FRIENDS

I AM KIND TO MYSELF AND OTHERS

I AM CREATING A MAGNIFICENT LIFE

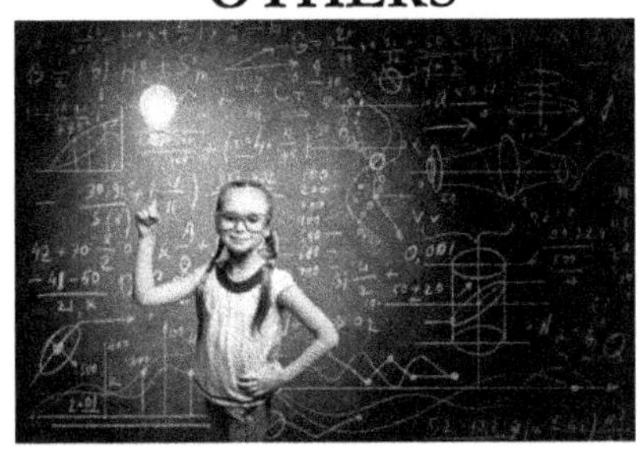

I AM GOOD AT WHATEVER I PUT MY MIND TO

I CHOOSE TO HOLD MY HEAD UP HIGH

PLEASE THANK YOU SORRY

I ALWAYS USE GOOD MANNERS

I TREAT OTHERS THE WAY I LIKE TO BE TREATED

I HAVE LOTS OF FUN EVER DAY

I FEEL FAB-U-LOUS

I AM IN CONTROL OF MY LIFE

I AM CREATING MY FUTURE NOW

I ALWAYS TRY MY BEST

I FEEL FANTASTIC

I FEEL AWESOME

I BELIEVE IN ME, YES I DO

I AM ON TOP OF THE WORLD

I LOVE AND APPRECIATE THE EARTH

I DESERVE ALL GOOD THINGS

I AM CONTENT

I LOVE TO USE MY IMAGINATION WHEN I DRAW

I LOVE TO SING FROM MY HEART

I LOVE TO DANCE LIKE NO ONE IS WATCHING

I LOVE TO USE MY IMAGINATION WHEN I PLAY

I LOVE TO SKIP

I AM EXACTLY WHERE I NEED TO BE

I LOVE TO RUN FAST LIKE THE WIND

I AM PROUD TO BE DIFFERENT

I LOVE TO EAT HEALTHY SNACKS

TEAMWORK MAKES THE DREAMWORK

GOOD THINGS HAPPEN TO ME

I MAKE GOOD CHOICES

I VALUE MY FRIENDSHIPS

I AM HEALTHY

I AM WEALTHY

EVERY LITTLE CELL IN MY BODY IS HAPPY

EVERY LITTLE CELL IN MY BODY IS WELL

I APPRECIATE OTHERS

I AM FILLED WITH COURAGE

I AM ENERGETIC

I ALWAYS TELL THE TRUTH

I WAKE UP HAPPY IN THE MORNING

I GO TO BED HAPPY & ON TIME

I HAVE A POSITIVE MINDSET

I LOVE EVERYTHING ABOUT MYSELF

I WORK WELL IN A TEAM

I WORK WELL ON MY OWN

THINK BIG IS A PIECE OF CAKE

I KNOW WHO I AM

I AM AMBITIOUS

I WELCOME SUCCESS WITH OPEN ARMS

I AM SURROUNDED BY ABUNDANCE

I WELCOME PROPRIETY WITH OPEN ARMS

MY MIND IS A POSITIVITY MAGNET

I AM INCREDIBLE

MY TIME IS PRECIOUS

I FOCUS ON POSITIVE CHANGE

I AM GOOD AT RECYCLING

EVERYDAY IS A NEW OPPORTUNITY

GOOD THINGS COME TO ME DAILY

MY PERSPECTIVE CHANGES EVERYTHING

I AM DESTINED FOR GREATNESS

I CHOOSE TO SMILE

I HAVE MANY SACRED GIFTS

WITH FAITH I CAN MOVE ANYTHING

I AM JOYFUL

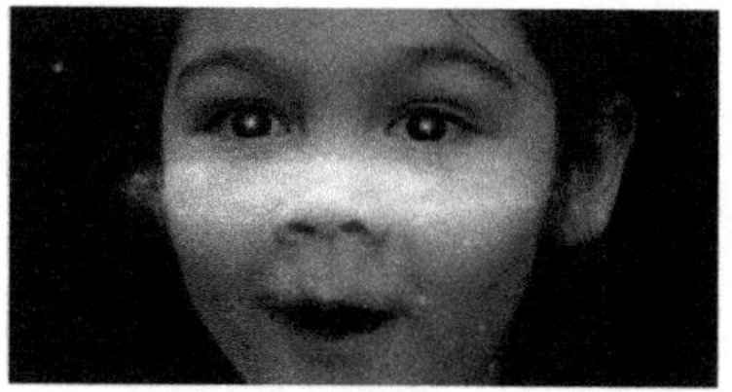

I AM DIVINE PERFECTION

**THANK YOU!
THANK YOU!
THANK YOU!**

I AM MY PRIORITY

**I APOLOGISE FOR MY MISTAKES
"I AM SORRY"**

I AM PROUD OF MYSELF

STICKY SITUATIONS CAN BE FUN

I MAKES MISTAKES SOMETIMES & WHEN I DO I CHOOSE TO FORGIVE MYSELF

EACH ONE OF US IS A BEAUTIFUL GIFT TO THE WOLRD

I CHOOSE TO LIVE EACH DAY WITH PURPOSE

PEACE BEGINS INSIDE EACH ONE OF US

I AM DESTINE TO DO GREAT THINGS

I AM EXPANDING

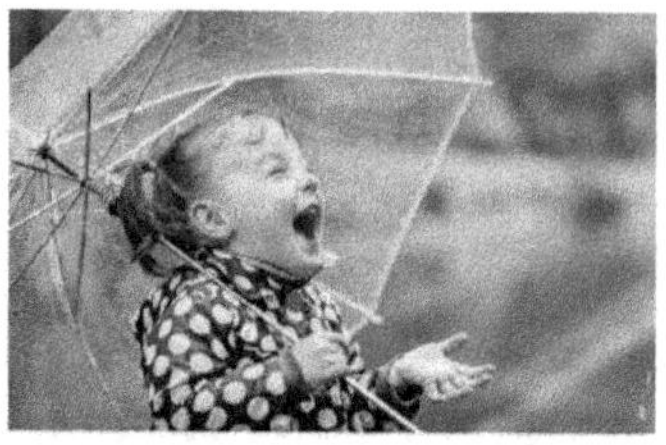

I CHOOSE TRUST THE PROCESS

IF AT FIRST I FAIL, I SIMPLY TRY AGAIN

I CHOOSE TO CREATE PEACE

WINNERS NEVER QUIT & QUITER NEVER WIN

I AM A PART OF THE SOLUTION

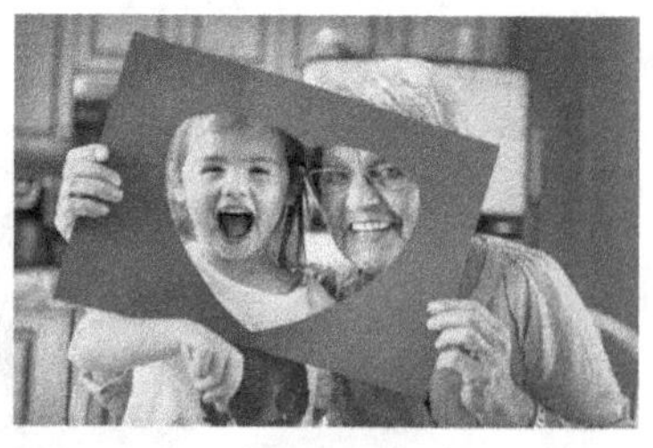

I AM FILLED WITH LOVE

I AM FILLED WITH JOY

I AM IN FLOW

I HAVE ENDLESS OPPORTUNITIES

I KEEP TRYING UNTIL I SUCCEED

READING FEEDS MY MIND

I RELEASE FEAR & WELCOME COURAGE

I AM THANKFUL FOR THE ABUNDANCE OF OPPORTUNITIES IN MY LIFE

I AM CENTERED

I AM WISE

I TRUST MYSELF

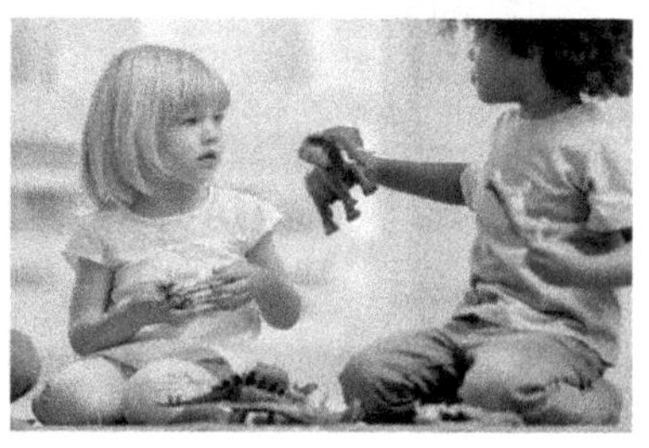

I AM IN HARMONY

I TREAT MYSELF AND OTHERS WITH KINDNESS

I GIVE MYAELF PERMISSION TO SHINE

I LOVE WHEN OTHER PEOPLE CHOOSE TO SHINE

I LOVE WHEN OTHER PEOPLE CHOOSE TO BE HAPPY

I TRUST MY FEELINGS

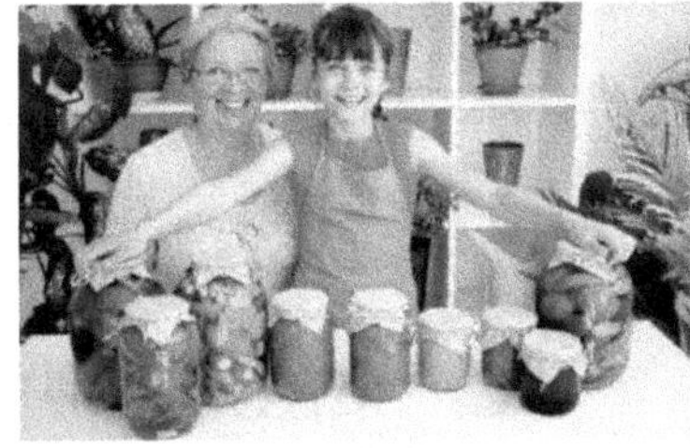

I ENJOY SPENDING TIME ON MY OWN & WITH OTHERS

MY OPINION MATTERS

PEOPLE LISTEN TO WHAT I HAVE TO SAY

I VALUE OTHER PEOPLES OPINION

I AM ONE OF A KIND

I AM UNIQUE

I RESPECTFULLY ASK FOR HELP WHEN NEEDED

I CELEBRATE MYSELF

I CELEBRATE OTHERS

I CHOOSE TO LEARN WHEN I AM CORRECTED

I SHOW MY FAMILY HOW MUCH I LOVE THEM

I SHOW MY FRIENDS HOW MUCH I APPRECIATE THEM

MY FAMILY ARE A GIFT TO ME

MY FRIENDS ARE A GIFT TO ME

I TAKE TIME TO SHOW OTHERS THAT I CARE

I SLEEP PEACEFULLY

I AM COMPASSIONATE TOWARDS ANIMALS

I AM COMPASSIONATE TOWARDS OTHERS

ALL IS WELL

I AM SAFE AND SUPPORTED

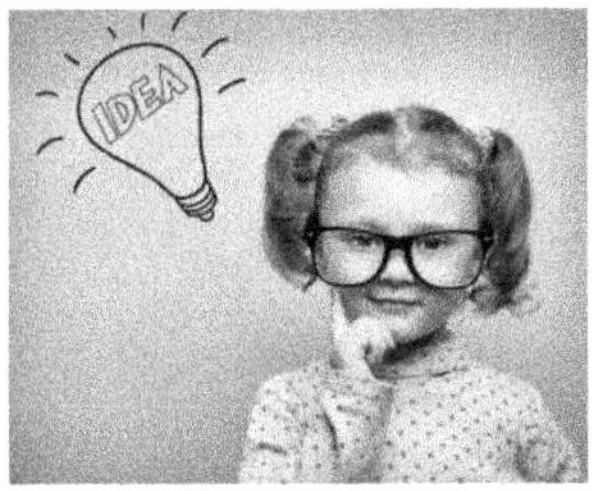

ALL PROBLEMS HAVE SOLUTIONS

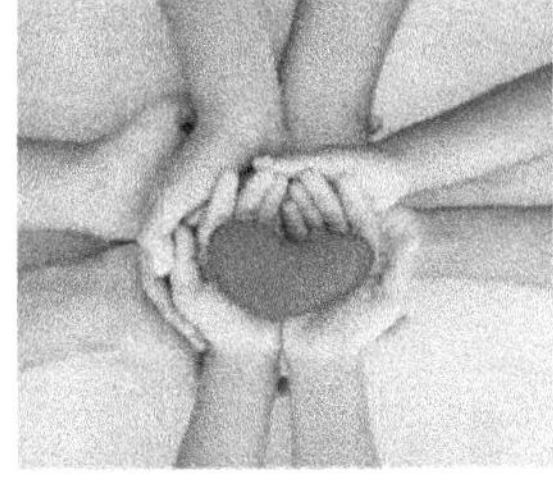

I MAKE OTHERS FEEL VALUED

ALL THAT I NEED COMES TO ME WITH EASE

I ALWAYS LISTEN TO MY HEART

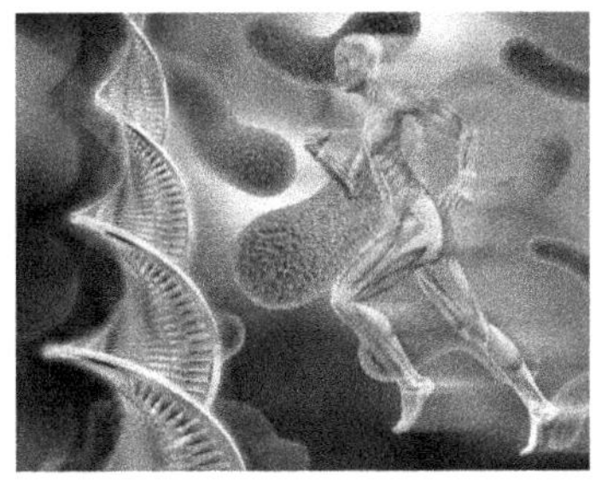

I APPRECIATE THE TRILLIONS OF CELLS IN MY BODY

MY DREAMS ALWAYS COME TRUE

I AM FRIENDLY

I CAN DO IT

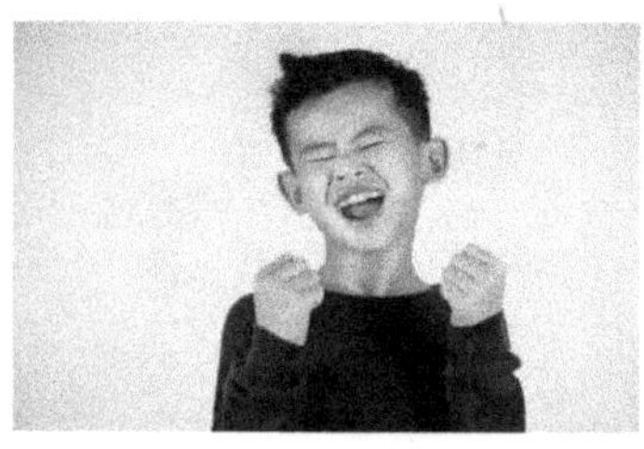

I CHOOSE TO FOLLOW MY BLISS

I AM GENEROUS

I AM PROTECTED

I AM GOOD AT SOLVING PROBLEMS

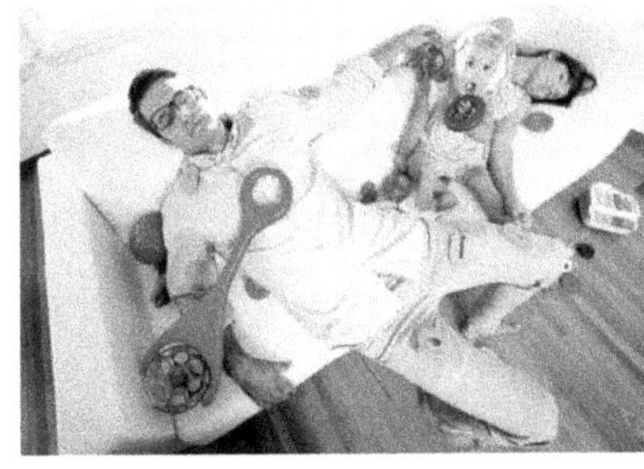

I HAVE LOTS OF ENERGY

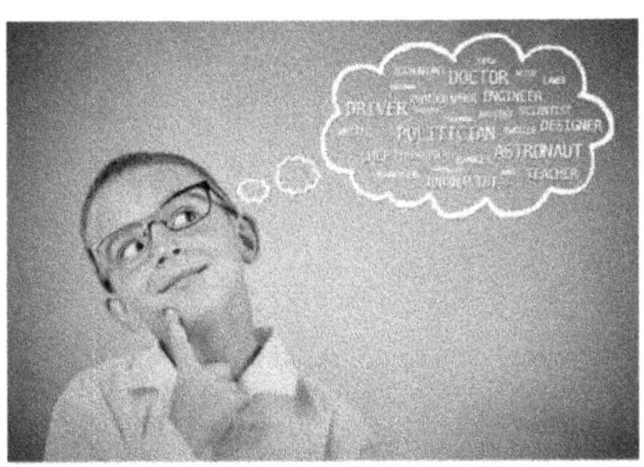

I CAN BECOME WHATEVER I WANT TO BE

I EMBRACE CHANGE

I MAKE FRIENDS EASILY

I AM CONTRIBUTING

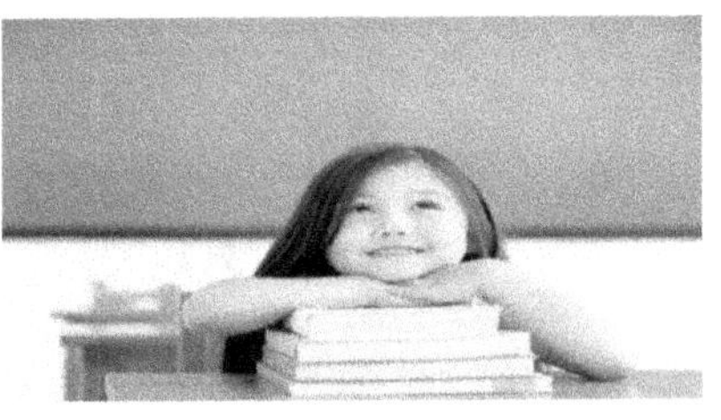

I HAVE HAPPY THOUGHTS

I FORGIVE OTHERS FOR THEIR MISTAKES

I AM FREE

I AM PERSISTENT

FREE WILL IS MY BIRTHRIGHT

I AM TRUSTWORTHY

I AM GENTLE

I AM PATIENT

LIFE IS FUN

KNOWLEDGE OPENS THE DOOR TO MY FUTURE

I LIKE BEING CHALLENGED

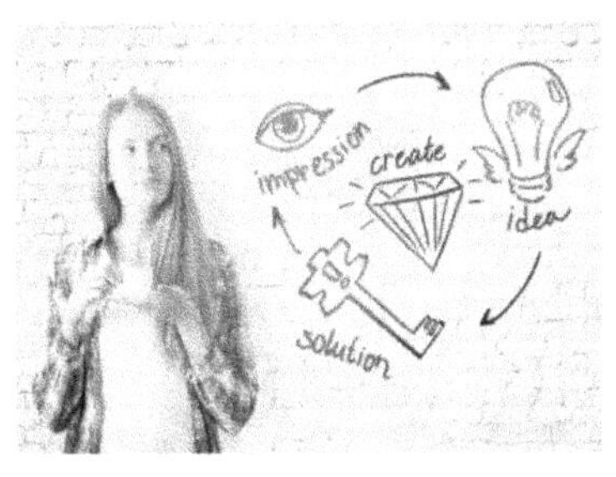

I AM OPTIMISTIC

I AM EXCITED ABOUT THE UNKNOWN

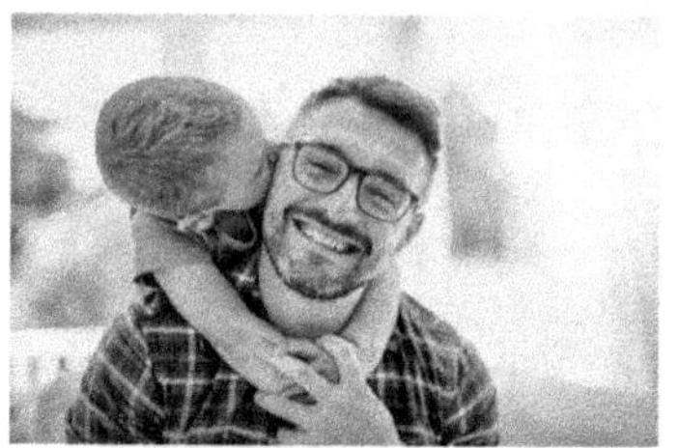

RESPECT IS IMPORTANT

I RECEIVE ALL THE HELP I NEED

AWESOME THINGS HAPPEN TO ME, FAMILY & FRIENDS

I BELIEVE IN MY DREAMS

I AM AN ACTION TAKER

I APPRECIATE EVERYONE IN MY LIFE

I CAN DO WHATEVER I FOCUS MY MIND ON

I AM A FAST LEARNER

LEARNING NEW THINGS IS FUN AND EXCITING

I CAN SEE THE BIGGER PICTURE

I AM POTENTIAL

I BELIEVE IN MIRACLES

I GET BETTER WITH PRACTICE

I LOVE TO WRITE STORIES

I LOVE MY FAMILY & MY HOME

I LOVE BEING SMART

I LOVE TO EAT VEGETABLES

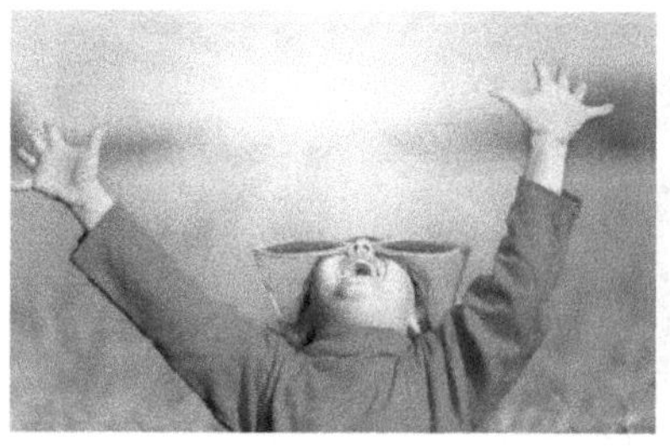

I LOVE MY LIFE SOOOO MUCH

MY MIND IS FILLED WITH AMAZING THINGS

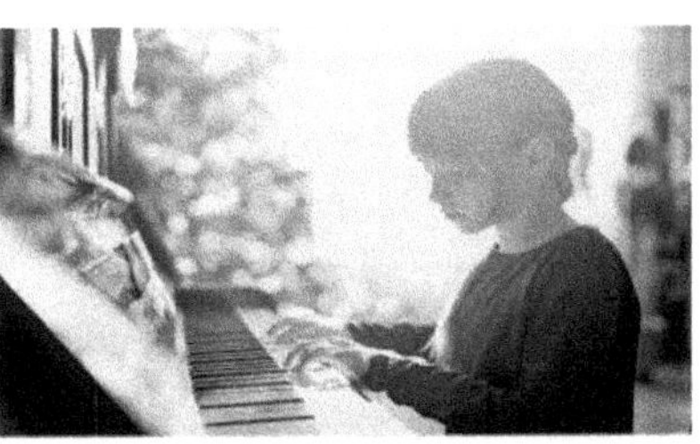

PLAY IS PRACTICE

I ACHIEVE EXTRAORDINARY RESULTS

I SEE BEAUTY EVERYWHERE I GO

MY IMAGINATION BEYOND AWESOME

I APPRECIATE TECHNOLOGY

I LOVE SCIENCE

I CAN CHOOSE TO HAVE FUN ALL DAY LONG

I AM A SUPER HERO

I LIKE TO DISCOVER NEW PLACES

I LOVE LEARNING EVERYDAY

I LOVE MATHS

I AM EXCELLENT AT ENGLISH

I AM EXCELLENT AT SCIENCE

I AM EXCELLENT AT HISTORY

I AM EXCELLENT AT GEOGRAPHY

I AM EXCELLENT AT SPORTS

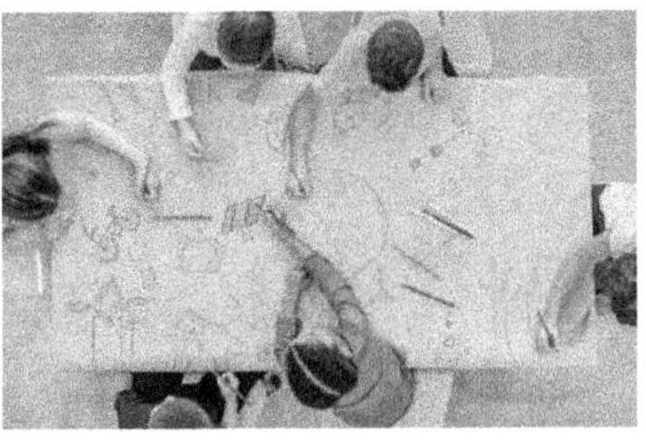

I AM EXCELLENT AT ART

MY IMAGINATION MAKES LIFE FUN

I LOVE MUSIC

I ENJOY DOING MY HOMEWORK

I JUMP FOR JOY IN LIFE

I CHOOSE TO FOCUS ON MY DREAMS

I RUN FREE WITH MY FRIENDS

I LOVE TO LEARN DIFFERENT LANGUAGES

I CHOOSE TO TOUCH THE WORLD WITH LOVE, PEACE AND KINDNESS

READING IS THE DIFFERENCE THAT MAKES THE DIFFERENCE

I APPRECIATE NATURE, IT IS BEAUTIFUL

IT FEELS GOOD TO GIVE

I AM INTELLIGENT & MIGHTY

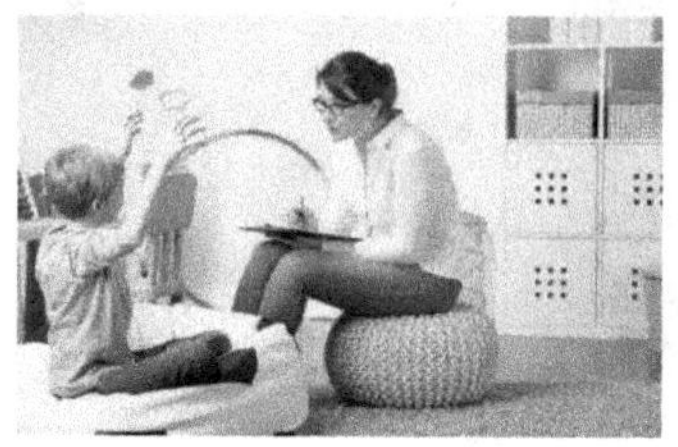

FAMILIES THAT PLAY TOGETHER, STAY TOGETHER

I AM WORKING ON MY FUTURE

I CAN SEE BEAUTY THROUGH MY WINDOW

I BELIEVE THAT SOMETHING AWESOME IS ABOUT TO HAPPEN

FAMILY IS THE CENTER OF MY WOLRD

I BELIEVE IN MYSELF, BECAUSE I HAVE THE POWER TO ACHIEVE

I AM A BEST SELLING AUTHOR

I CAN SEE FURTHER ON THE SHOULDERS OF GIANTS

THERE IS ALWAYS FUN THINGS TO DO OUTSIDE

I CAN BECOME A DRUMMER WHEN I USE MY IMAGINATION

I ENJOY TIME WITH FRIENDS IN NATURE

I LEARN BEST WHEN I'M HAPPY

I ENJOY SAVING MONEY

I AM STRONG

I SAY "MAY I BE EXCUSED" WHEN I FINISH EATING

I ASK BEFORE I TOUCH SOMEONE ELSES BELONGINGS

I LOVE KNOWING THAT ALL IS WELL

I ENJOY HAVING FUN LEARNING WITH MY FRIENDS

I ENJOY TAKING CARE OF OUR ENVIRONMENT

I AM A UNIQUE PIECE TO THE PUZZLE

I ONLY NEED TO TAKE ONE STEP AT A TIME

THERE IS ALWAYS SPACE FOR IMPROVEMENT

I MAKE SPACE FOR GROWTH

I CHOOSE TO SOAR LIKE AN EGALE

I WELCOME FEEDBACK

I LIKE TO ASK QUESTIONS

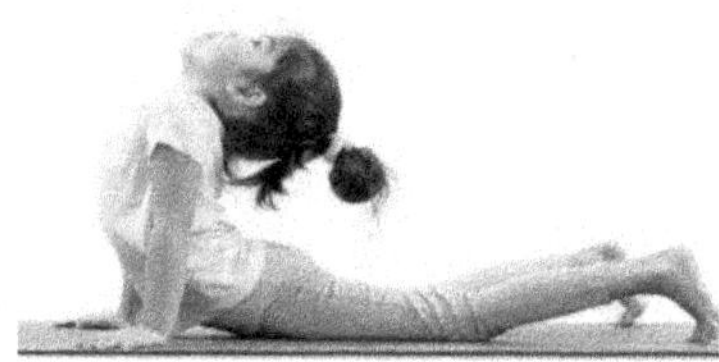

I LOVE MY BODY

I LOVE TO LAUGH

I CAN CHOOSE TO BE IN THE CHOICE

SHIFT HAPPENS CONSTANTLY

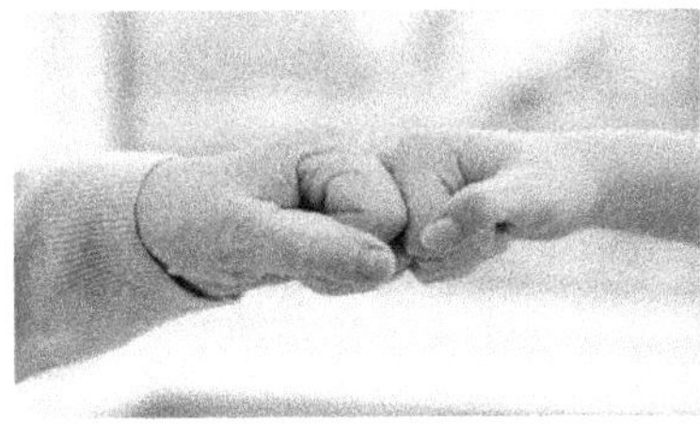

I TREAT OTHERS THE WAY I LIKE TO BE TREATED

IT IS POSSIBLE, ONE SEED AT A TIME

I CHOOSE TO BELIEVE THAT THE IMPOSSIBLE IS POSSIBLE

THOUGHTS BECOME THINGS

TOGETHER ANYTHING IS POSSIBLE

I HAVE A DREAM

I CAN CHANGE THE WORLD ONE THOUGHT AT A TIME

I AM A GOOD ROLE MODEL

ALL OF LIFE SUPPORTS ME

CREATIVITY IS MY NATURAL STATE

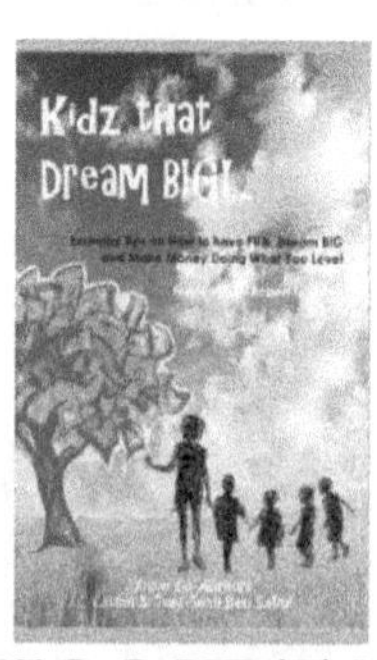

I CHOOSE TO BE THE CHANGE I WANT TO SEE IN THE WORLD

I AM FORTUNATE

I AM ENERGY

I LOVE MULTIMILLIONAIRE

I AM EDUCATED

I AM CHARITABLE

I AM FEEDING MY MIND

I AM A PHILANTHROPIST

I AM
INFINITE

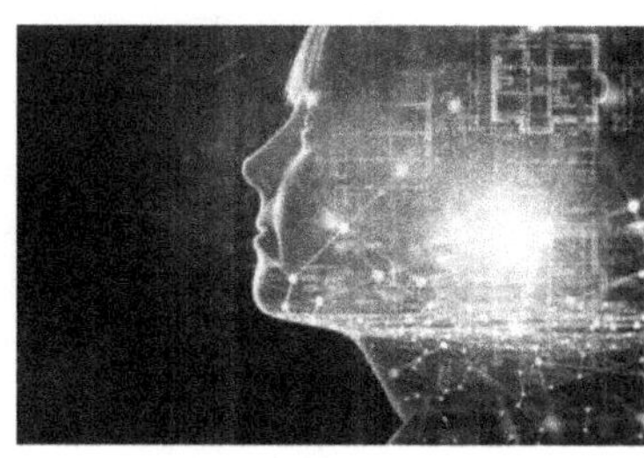

I AM
IMMEASURABLE

I AM
OUTSTANDING

I AM A WAKING UP
TO
MY DREAMS
& ASPIRATIONS

I AM A
GO GETTER

WELL DONE FOR READING THE 365 AFFIRMATIONS.
PLEASE LEAVE A REVIEW FOR THE BOOK ON AMAZON

YOU ARE AWESOME

NOW MY FAMILY
ARE GOING TO SHARE
SOME BONOUS INFORMATION
WITH YOU

CREATE YOUR OWN AFFIRMATIONS

Did you know that affirmations as simply belief statements. So you can choose to have a negative belief or a positive belief about yourself and others.

To create your own positive affirmation simply choose one negative thought and then simply come up with a positive one to counteract the negative one.

For example "I never get things right."

Then your new belief could be "There's no such thing as failure, only feedback."

Make your affirmations short so they're easier for you to remember.

1) ____
2) ____
3) ____
4) ____
5) ____
6) ____
7) ____
8) ____
9) ____
10) ____

ABOUT THE AUTHOR

AMIRE BEN SALMI

So much for saying "You're too young"

Amire Ben Salmi is a 4 years old public speaker, author and founder of his brand called "Because I AM Intelligent". He sells T-Shits, Cars, Books and Affirmation Cards. If Amire can do it, that means you can too.

Amire aims to inspire children from around the world to celebrate their uniqueness and go after their Dreams and Aspirations. Amire enjoys playing football, running, drawing, playing with his siblings and friends, travelling, eating ice cream, going on trains and visiting places like Legoland and Chessington World of Adventures.

Amire is the youngest of five siblings: 17YR OLD LASHAI, 13YR OLD TRAY-SEAN, 10YR OLD YASMINE and 8YR OLDPAOLO

Together they are known as

"The Fantastic Five"

Surprise Bonus: DID YOU KNOW?

Did YOU know that we all develop our belief systems about ourselves and the world around us from our environment?

Our family and friends, role models, television, magazines and advertising can either be nurturing or damaging.

It is important that we, our families and our friends learn to take control of our belief systems and the younger that we do, the easier it is.

It can be as simple as affirming the positive beliefs that we would like to grow up with. Negative beliefs can impact our lives greatly and can be hard to shift as we grow older. Affirmations are a powerful and holistic way of building positive mind and happier children and will go onto help them through their lives.

This will also nurture their authentic self and help them to enjoy the magic of childhood. Put simply, Because I Am Intelligent - 365 Affirmations To Brighten Up Your Day aims to affirm to one's self positive words that are absorbed by the mind to create your belief system.
Once affirmations are learned, they work by coming to mind when that belief is challenged.

For example if your affirmation is
"I am wonderful just the way I am",
and you are told you are stupid,
the affirmation will come to mind to remind you of your belief.

Instead, you will think, "I'm not stupid, I am wonderful!"

Without a positive belief, you may take on the one you just heard and start to believe that you are stupid.
The more an affirmation is repeated, positive or negative, the stronger it becomes.

ABOUT THE BEN SALMI FAMILY

BYA Mother of The Year Award Winner

Sabrina Ben Salmi BSc

Is a proud mother of
5 Entrepreneurial children aged 4 to 17years old who she referees to as her
Fantastic 5.

Sabrina is a Multi-Award Winning Author, Business & Personal Development Consultant, Founding directors of an Ofsted rated Outstanding school: Harris Invictus Academy (Secondary).
Former Radio Show Host, Public Speaker. Founder of Dreaming Big Together Formula & 21 Day Shift Happens.

Sabrina Ben Salmi BSc is here to empower you to plant the seed so that you and your family can learn to Dream Big Together via a variety of products and services that aim to assist you and your loved ones to create a brighter future. Sabrina and her children have been featured in the media Internationally via Radio, TV, Newspapers, magazines etc to name a few Channel 4 documentaries:
Secret Millionaire/Child Genius, BBC London News, LBC Radio, BBC Radio, Fabulous Magazine etc.

"It's about time that we stop granting our children indefinite leave to remain on the streets and empower them to plant the seed for a brighter tomorrow"

Mohamed Ben Salmi

Is a proud father of
5 Entrepreneurial children aged 4 to 17years old

Speaks Arabic/French/English, author of 'A Mirror of Happiness' and has a passion for music, travel, languages, meeting new people and biology.

Lashai Ben Salmi is a 17yr old

Multi-Award winning Youth Advocate, Winner of TruLittle Hero Award - Entrepreneur 2017, Speaker at Virgin Money Lounge Historical Black History Month first ever event, YouTuber 12K Subscribers plus, PRECIOUS Award Winner, Rotary Young Citizen Award, Award-Winning Author of Kidz That Dream Big & Kidz book series, Andy Harrington ACE Coach, Former International Radio Show Host, UnLTD Award Winner, Winner of Andy Harrington Public Speaking Awards x 2, Harry Singha Foundation Lead Coach, Winner of Regan Hillyer International Scholarship, Public Speaker,

Training, Short Film: I AM A Piece To The Puzzle, Business/Personal Developments Consultant and Founder of My Journey - Giving Youth Several Reasons to Smile.

She is here to help you to plant the seed for self realisation, personal development and happiness in abundance via a variety of products and services to assist you to create a brighter future.

- Mother & Daughter Discussions of Exploration

- Stepping Stones Coaching

- My Journey – Creating A Vision Board for My Future

- My Journey – Sharing My Message From The Stage

- My Journey - Inspiring My Community To Pay It Forward

- My Journey - There's A Book Inside ME

- Stepping Stones - Families That Play Together, Stay Together.

Tray-Sean Ben Salmi aka I'm That KID

is a 13yr old

Multi-Award Winning Child Advocate, participant of Child Genius 2017 1 of the final 20 smartest children in the UK, An Award Winning Author of Kidz That Dream Big book series, Former Radio Show Host, Regan Hillyer International Be Your Brand Fellow,

Author of 10 Seconds To Child Genius, Events Host, UnLTD Award winner, nominated for National Diversity Award, Winner of TruLittle Hero Award - Academic 2017, Public Speaker, Business/Personal Developments Consultant and Founder of I'm That KID which offers a variety of products and services:

- I'm That KID - Bridging The Gap Between Fathers & Sons

- I'm That KID – Wristbands, Keyrings & T-Shirts

- I'm That KID – Creating A Vision Board for My Future

- I'm That KID – Taking The Stage

- I'm That KID - Inspiring My Community To Pay It Forward

- I'm That KID - There's A Book Inside ME

- I'm That KID - Families That Play Together, Stay Together

- I'm That KID - Empowering You To Step Into Your POWER

And Co-Founder of 10 Seconds To Child Genius who is here to help children and youth to plant the seed for an abundance of unique opportunities via a variety of products and services to assist you to create a brighter future. My brother Tray-Sean Ben Salmi decided to get out of his comfort zone one day and applied to participate in Channel 4 TV 'Child Genius' competition competing against the best 8 – 12 years old in the UK and he managed to pass all their tests, interviews and assessments and made it to the Child Genius' 2017 Finals as one of the Top 20 contestants in the country.

We are so proud of him

Yasmine Ben Salmi aka LovePrenure

is an 10yr old

Award winning Author of The Choice is Your - 10 Keys Principles To Create A Happier Lifestyle, Winner of TruLittle Heros Award - Creative 2017, Former International Radio Show Host and founder of Loveprenure. Yasmine is here to help you to plant the seed for wealth, health and happiness in abundance via a variety of products and services to assist you to create a brighter future.

Paolo Ben Salmi aka Pint Size Adventurer

is 8yr old

He is an Award Winning Author of Pint Size Adventurer - 10 Keys Principles To Get Your KIDS off their iPads & Into The Wild, 2nd place in TruLittle Heros Award - U12 Entreprenur 2017, Former International Radio Show Host, 22/9/17

Paolo made history by being the youngest to interview **Dr JohnDemartini**:

https://www.facebook.com/350400542063654/videos/363072487463126/, personal developments coach and founder of Pint Size Adventurer who is here to help you to plant the seed toward self discovery, exploration of the internal and external world and adventurer in abundance via a variety of products and services to assist you to create a brighter future

Amire Ben Salmi aka Mr Because I AM Intelligent

is a 4yr old

An Award Winning Author of Because I AM Intelligent - 52 Affirmations To Brighten Up Your Day and founder of Because I AM Intelligent who is here to help you to plant the seed toward having fun learning during childhood, Positive Affirmations, Fun and Creativity in abundance via a variety of products such as a book with a matching colour car and 52 affirmation cards to assist you to create a brighter future.

YOU CAN CONNECT WITH ALL OF US ON FACEBOOK

OUR FAMILY BELIEFS & OUR FAMILY ANTHEM

We believe that there is no such thing as failure only feedback.

We also believe that the journey of one-thousand miles begins with a single step

Family Anthem:

If you want to be somebody,

If you want to go somewhere,

You better wake up and PAY ATTENTION

I'm ready to be somebody,

I'm ready to go somewhere,

I'm ready to wake up and PAY ATTENTION!

The question is ARE YOU

OUR NAN MARY PAUL

Our Nan Mary Paul is the founder of MARY PAUL.

She produces bespoke art and furniture for the high end market.

Mary became a single parent and her child (our mum) needed a lot of care due to childhood illnesses.

Our Nan had to juggle motherhood with 3 jobs and find time to pursue her passion. She launched a community project with the aim to get the community engaged.

Our Nanas furniture has been featured in the newspaper with the Queen of Jordan. Mary has exhibited her furniture in exhibitions such as Hidden Aart, 100% Design and Top Draw to name a few.

Mary has many dreams and desires to live the legacy and then leave a legacy for generations to come.

The inspiration behind MARY PAUL was to end, once and for all, what she saw as " the dubious concept of so called single parenthood".

Mary desired to make her mark and felt that expressing herself through the medium of art. Be that furniture, paintings, home staging, personal stylist that was the difference that made the difference for her and her clients. Mary is a family woman and is now a proud mother of one Daughter and 5 Grandchildren.

DID YOU KNOW THIS ABOUT YOUR AUTHOR?

Amire did not speak at all when he use to go on stage with his family for their Dreaming oh Together events. Until one day when

Amire asked his mum a question.

Amire "Mummy, So you know why I do not talk when I go on stage?"

Mum "No son, please tell me"

Amire "Because I don't have a BRAND like my brothers and sisters"

Mum "Oh wow Amire, thank you for sharing. Do you know what a brand is"

Amire **"Yes, it'a your message to the world"**

Mum "Oh wow, you are very smart Amire.

What would you like to call your brand"

Amire "Because I AM Intelligent"

Mum "Oh wow!

Amire you are beyond amazing.

I love the name of your new brand. Will you go on stage to speak now?"

Amire "Yes mum"

The next time Amire attended an event he went on stage and said

Amire "Hello my name is Amire Ben Salmi and

I am 4yrs old and my brand is called Because I AM Intelligent. I sell a book, T-shirts and cars"

So you see from a simply conversation a brand is born and to date Amire enjoys speaking to people about his brand and products.

THE AWESOME THING IS, NOW THAT YOU KNOW THAT AMIRE DID IT,

THAT MEANS YOU CAN TOO.

10 FACTS ABOUT YOUR BRAIN

FACT ONE:

There are always 4 Stages of Learning

Stage One – UNCONSCIOUS INCOMPETENCE

This is when you start doing something new by 'Trial and Error' and hoping it will work. Does it? Hmm!

Stage Two – CONSCIOUS INCOMPETENCE

This is the 'MAKE or BREAK' stage and often 95% people will give up at this stage if they don't get success quickly and as a consequence, they will NEVER discover their real potential.
So it is vital to get a Mentor, Coach or an Instructor.

For example, if you want to learn to drive a car then book a serious course of lessons with a Qualified Driving Instructor.

Stage Three – CONSCIOUS COMPETENCE

Yes! You can do it.
Like after a number of lessons you know how to drive a car but you still need to think of everything you are doing to drive the car safely!

Stage Four : UNCONSCIOUS COMPETENCE

You have Mastered the skill because you had so much practice and can do it without thinking about it.

FACT TWO:

We all have a Preferred Learning Style known as V.A.K.

V – VISUAL (We learn by Reading or Looking at the information)

A – AUDITORY (We learn by Listening or Talking)

K – KINESTHETICS (We learn by Doing and being Active)

To increase our skills factor, ideally we want to develop over time all three styles V, A and K.

FACT THREE:

We actually have five Types of W.I.R.E.S. Memory.

W – WORKING MEMORY (Short Term Memory)

I – IMPLICIT MEMORY (Or sometimes called 'The Muscle' memory. Once you have learned to do something, like how to use a new computer software etc.)

R – REMOTE (This is your lifetime accumulation of skills and knowledge and seems to diminish with age if you don't use it. "USE IT or LOSE IT")

E – EPISODIC (This is when you have a memory of a specific experience or an event.)

S - SEMANTIC (This is when certain words and symbols are special to the individual.)

FACT FOUR:

Learn to Search and Recognize Patterns

that enhance Brain development.

FACT FIVE:

Your ability to learn is 'State' dependent So have a High Expectation - when you learn you will succeed.

FACT SIX:

Emotions and Learning are closely linked.

Watch what you are saying to yourself when learning.
Have a high expectation of yourself.

Don't say :
"I will never be able to learn all these things"

Instead, say something like:

"Everything I learn I will remember at the right time to use it."

FACT SEVEN:

We all have 'DUAL' Daily Learning cycles

The two cycles are :
"Low to high energy" and "Relaxation to Tension" Cycle.
So be aware of your best time for learning, especially for test revision.

FACT EIGHT:

Our brain modal switches over roughly every 90 minutes.

Generally speaking, our left brain is more efficient for verbal skills and our right brain for spatial skills.

FACT NINE:

Our Learning and Physical performance is affected by our biological rhythms throughout the day .

Even our breathing has cycles.
Overall, short term memory is best in the morning and not so effective in the afternoon.
Whilst our long term memory is better in the afternoon.

FACT TEN:

Your brain needs Deep Relaxing sleep.

This allows time for your brain to process all the things you have learned.
Getting into a REM sleep (Dreaming) has been found by researchers to be very important for learning.

KEEP IN TOUCH WITH 4yr old AMIRE VIA SOCIAL MEDIA:

YouTube: Amire Ben Salmi

Twitter: @AmireBenSalmi

Facebook: Because I AM Intelligent

PLEASE LEAVE A REVIEW FOR THIS BOOK ON AMAZON, THANK YOU IN ADVANCE.

SURPRISE BONUS

THIS IS YOUR OPPORTUNITY TO MAKE YOUR STATEMENT

THINK BIG…THINK BOLD BECAUSE YOU ARE AWESOME AND I BELIEVE IN YOU

Make your statement below :

I AM AMAZING BECAUSE…………………

____

____

Stick a passport size photo of yourself smiling on the X below:

X

With love from Amire Ben Salmi

SURPRISE ACTIVITIES

GOING TO SCHOOL MAZE

Help Hank get to school!
Trace the fastest route to get to school.

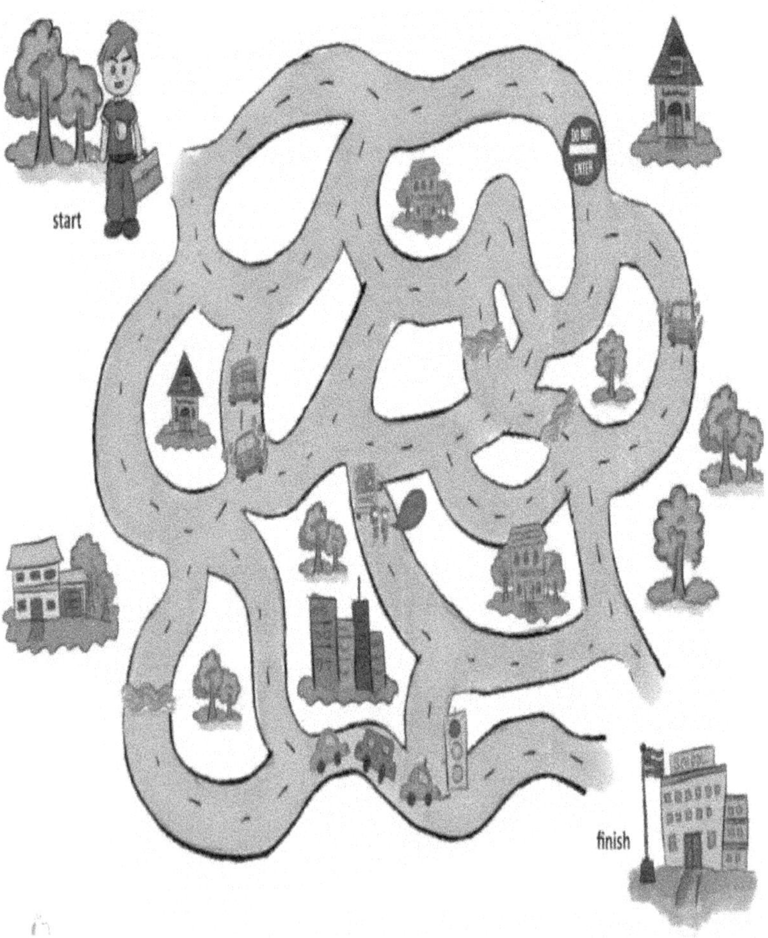

GUIDE CHARTWELL THE ADVENTURER THROUGH
THE CLIFF MAZE TO THE TREASURE CHEST BELOW.

Aa

It's time to pick apples! Draw a path from the apple to the hand by following the letter A.

b	C	d	e	F	G	h	i	J	k	L	M	n	A	o
v	U	t	S	r	Q	A	a	A	a	A	a	A	a	P
W	A	a	A	a	x	a	Y	z	B	c	D	e	F	G
L	a	K	j	A	i	A	a	A	a	A	a	A	a	h
m	A	n	O	a	P	q	R	s	T	u	V	w	A	x
C	a	B	z	A	a	A	a	A	a	A	a	A	a	Y
d	A	e	F	g	H	i	J	k	L	m	N	o	P	q
X	a	A	a	A	w	V	u	T	s	A	a	A	a	R
y	Z	b	C	a	D	a	A	a	A	a	E	f	A	G
S	r	Q	p	A	o	A	n	M	I	K	j	l	a	H
t	A	a	A	a	U	a	V	w	X	y	Z	b	A	c
J	a	l	h	G	f	A	e	A	a	A	a	A	a	D
k	A	a	A	a	A	a	L	a	M	n	O	p	Q	r
g	F	e	D	c	B	z	y	A	x	W	v	U	t	S
H	i	J	k	L	m	N	o	a	P	q	R	s	T	u

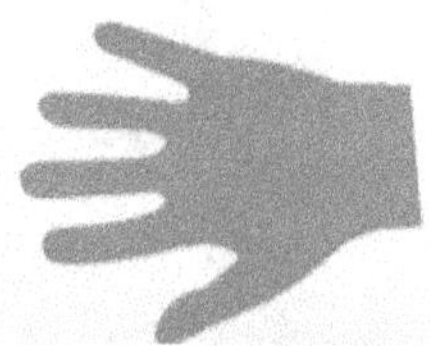

Follow the path from 1 to 20 and help Mama Bird get to the nest.

Saving Water

It is important to save water beacuse it helps plants, animals, and humans live.
Help save water by making sure that the faucet is off and not dripping!

Help Hydro turn off the leaky faucet!

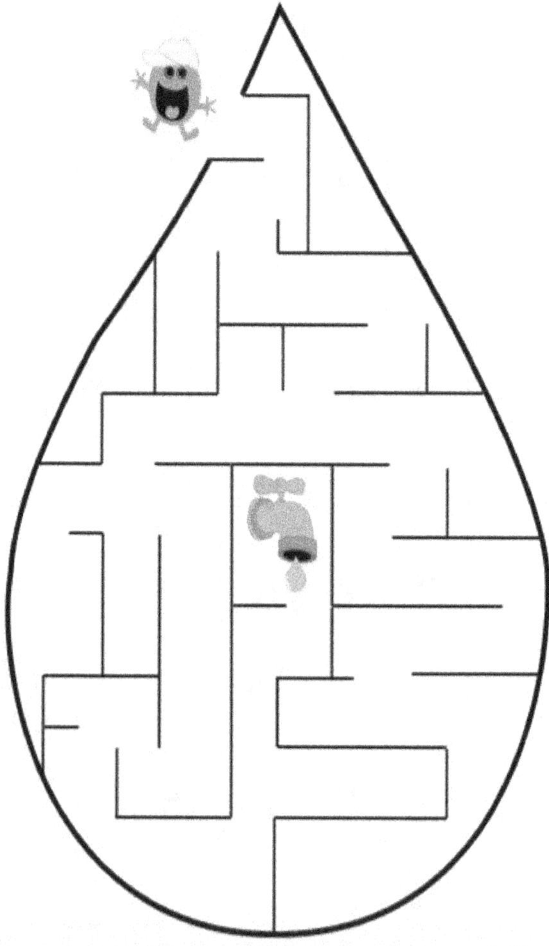

Follow the path from **A** to **K**.

RAPUNZEL'S RESCUE

Help Rapunzel's prince through the tower maze to rescue Rapunzel.

Calendar Maze

Find your way through the calendar pages to make it to the new year!

Short Vowel Review

a e i o u

Write the missing vowel for each word below.

b d

c t

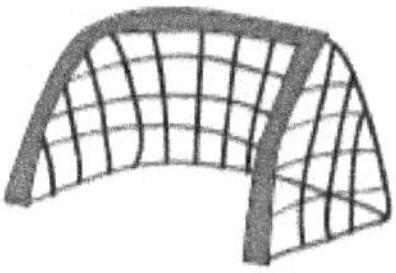

n t

n t

d g

b t

p g

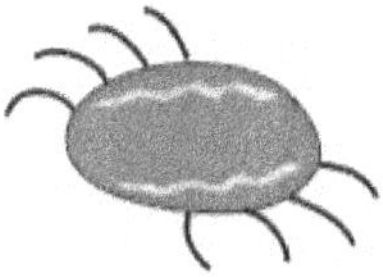

b g

t n

Beginning Blends 1

Fill in the blanks with the correct consonant blend.

_ _ead

_ _og

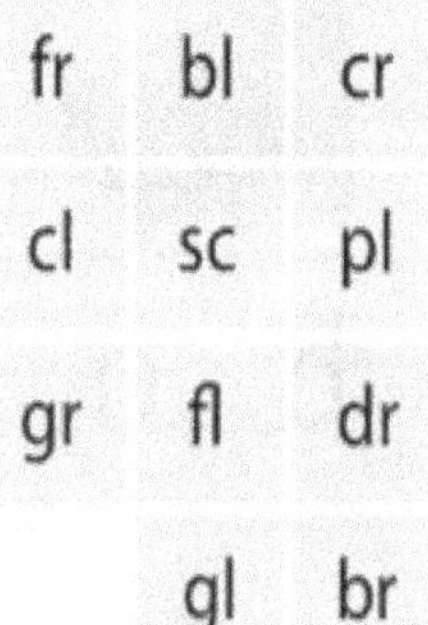

fr	bl	cr
cl	sc	pl
gr	fl	dr
	gl	br

_ _oud

_ _y

_ _ant

_ _ock

_ _ue

_ _ab

_ _ush

_ _anket

_ _apes

_ _um

_ _ale

write a crazy SUMMER story!

Fill in this story with names of your summer friends and the correct parts of speech to come up with a truly outrageous story. Maybe some day this experience will happen to you!

One day, ________ (NAME 1) and ________ (NAME 2) decided to ________ (VERB) while on their summer vacation. ________ (NAME 1) grabbed a ________ (NOUN) and hit the road! ________ (NAME 1) thought they should ________ (VERB) which ________ (NAME 2) thought was very wild. "It's summer vacation! We have to ________ (VERB)!" ________ (NAME 1) exclaimed. While on their journey ________ (NAME 1) saw a ________ (ANIMAL) climbing a ________ (NOUN) and that scared ________ (NAME 2). Later, it was time for a snack so ________ (NAME 2) suggested they eat ________ (TYPE OF FOOD) and ________ (TYPE OF FOOD) and drink ________ (TYPE OF FOOD) juice. Summertime is all about ________ (ADJECTIVE) experiences, and ________ (NAME 1) and ________ (NAME 2) wanted to make the most of it. After a quick ________ (VERB) in the ________ (BODY OF WATER), it was time to ________ (VERB). It had been another ________ (ADJECTIVE) summer day!

S Blends

Read these words aloud. Listen for the **letter blend**, or combination of sounds, at the beginning of the word.

Say the name of the picture out loud. Circle the letters that make the beginning sound.

 st sm	 sp sl	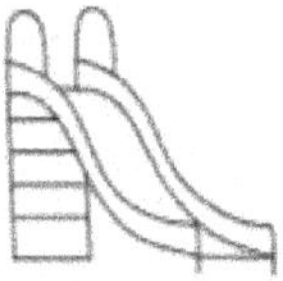 sl sw
 sn st	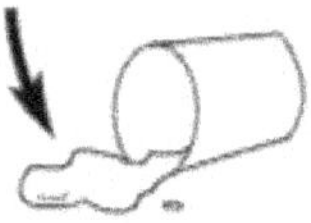 sm sp	 st sc
 sw sp	 sk st	 sp sw
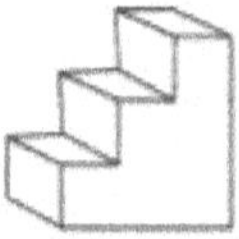 sc st	 sp sn	 sl sm

Months of the Year

Name______________________________ Date________________

Read each clue. Write the answer.

January	February	March	April	May	June	July
August	September	October	November	December		

1. First month of the year ___January___
2. Last month of the year ____________
3. Month after June ____________
4. Month before September ____________
5. Month between May and July ____________
6. Second month of the year ____________
7. Tenth month of the year ____________
8. Third month of the year ____________
9. Month between March and May ____________
10. Fifth month of the year ____________
11. Month before October ____________
12. Month before December ____________

Your Body

Name each part of your body in the space below.

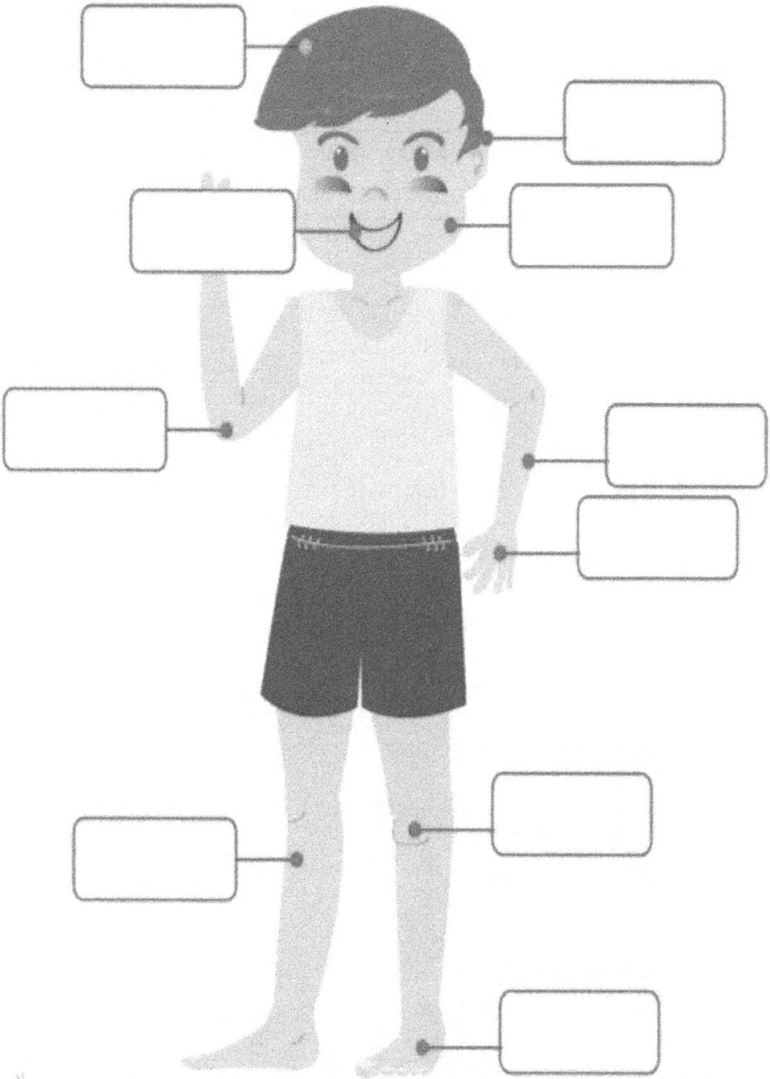

Name Date

FIND THE MISSING LETTER

Letters are missing below! Use the pictures as clues to find the missing letter.

1. The __abbit sees a __arrot.

2. A __loud covers the __un.

3. The __og chases the __at.

4. __ows eat __rass on the farm.

5. The __ug crawls on a __lower.

6. I like __ooks about __hosts.

Connect the dots and Color!
Smiling Lion

www.ingramcontent.com/pod-product-compliance
Lightning Source LLC
Chambersburg PA
CBHW071053090426
42737CB00013B/2339

* 9 7 8 1 9 1 2 5 4 7 0 2 9 *